THE STAR WARS COOKBOOK

ICE SABERS

30 CHILLED TREATS USING THE FORCE OF YOUR FREEZER

BY LARA STARR

PHOTOGRAPHY BY MATTHEW CARDEN

chronicle books · san francisco

ISBN: 978-1-4521-0761-5

Figures and vehicles courtesy of Hasbro, Galoob, and Applause.

Tootsie Rolls are a registered trademark of Tootsie Roll Industries, Inc.
Moose Tracks is a registered trademark of Denali Flavors, Inc.

Book design by Jennifer Tolo Pierce.
Art direction and concepts by Matthew Carden.
Styling by Jennifer Carden.
Typeset in Bell Gothic, Clicker, Interstate, and Univers.

Manufactured in China.

10 9 8 7 6 5 4 3

Chronicle Books LLC
680 Second Street, San Francisco, California 94107

www.chroniclekids.com
www.starwars.com

Table of Contents

Introduction

May the Force of your freezer be with you!

The Force is present everywhere, including the kitchen. Its power is as present in your freezer as it is on Hoth. With these recipes and your new lightsaber (ice saber) ice-pop molds, your culinary creations will be filled with the Force.

Some of these recipes are simple enough to make on your own and enjoy with friends. There are others requiring the help of an adult. Be sure to get your parents or other grown-ups involved. Seek the wisdom of their cooking experience.

As you venture into the kitchen, you will want the sagacity of this cookbook and the power of the lightsaber ice-pop molds to help guide your way. Adventure and tastiness will be yours as you create these recipes for those who hunger for them. Accept the challenge, young Padawan, and feel the Force!

GETTING STARTED

Before you start making these recipes, you must master some essential safety steps. The kitchen is a realm of peace, yet danger lurks in the most ordinary-seeming places. The three most important rules to remember are:

1. Keep an adult in the kitchen at all times, especially when you use knives, the stovetop, or the oven. Adults make good company and are helpful and handy to have around. (Even Luke would have been toast without Ben Kenobi to guide and protect him.) They can reach high places, drive, use the phone, pay, and offer valuable advice. Remember, never use anything sharp or hot without an adult to guide you.

2. Wash your hands with soap and warm water before cooking. You remember the hideous creatures in the Mos Eisley Cantina? They are nothing compared to what are crawling around on your hands. Fight those microscopic life forms with your best weapons: soap and water. It's a good idea to wash your hands a few times while you're cooking, too, as the germ troops are known to send in constant reinforcements.

3. Wash the ice-pop molds in warm, soapy water before you use them the first time.

....

The calm and perceptive mind of a Jedi warrior will enable you to prevent most mishaps in the kitchen. Use it well and follow these general guidelines:

BE CAREFUL
Respect the mysteries of the Force

Freezing time will vary. For quickest results, place your frozen treats toward the back of the freezer and open the door as few times as possible during the freezing time.

To release the ice sabers from the molds, allow them to thaw on the counter for 3 to 5 minutes or run them under hot water for 5 seconds on each side.

► Never run in the kitchen.

► Keep everything—pot holders, towels, packages of ingredients, this book—away from burners on the stove. The stove can be hot even if the burners are all turned off.

► Dry your hands before turning on any electric switch or putting in or pulling out a plug.

► Wash knives and other sharp utensils one at a time. Don't drop them in a pan or bucket of soapy water—you may cut yourself when you reach in to fish them out.

► Lift lids on hot pots at an angle away from you, directing the rising steam away from your face.

► Use only dry pot holders. Wet ones will give you a steam burn when you touch the handle of a hot pot.

► Put a pot or pan on the stove before you turn on the heat.

► Turn off the heat before you remove a pot or pan from the stove.

► Never put out a grease fire with water. Water causes grease to splatter and can spread the fire very quickly. To put out a grease fire, smother it with a tight-fitting lid or throw handfuls of baking soda onto it.

BE AWARE
Cultivate the awareness of a Jedi

► Never leave the kitchen while something is cooking on the stove or in the oven.

► Keep pot handles away from the edge of the stove so no one passing by topples the pot.

► Always position pot handles away from other stove burners. Otherwise, they'll get hot and burn you when you move the pot.

► Remove utensils from hot pots when you're not using them, placing them on a plate or spoon holder near the stove. Metal spoons and spatulas are especially dangerous, because they'll absorb and hold the heat and burn your hand when you go to use them.

► Start with a clean kitchen and keep it clean as you cook. When something spills, wipe it up immediately to keep accidents from happening. If you have time, wash dishes as you go.

► Turn off the blender's motor before removing the lid.

► Put ingredients away when you're finished with them.

► Know where to find the fire extinguisher and be sure it's in working order.

► Keep the fire department number next to the phone.

The tools of a Jedi chef are powerful but simple. You probably already have everything in your kitchen. Here's an alphabetical list of what you may need:

EQUIPMENT
Aluminum foil
Baking dishes
Baking sheets
Blender*
Can opener
Candy thermometer*
Cheese grater*
Colander
Cookie cutters
Cooling rack
Cutting board
Electric mixer*
Food coloring pen
Ice cream maker
Ice cream scoop
Ice cream sundae bowls
Ice cube tray
Ice-pop sticks
Knives* (one large and one small)
Lollipop sticks
Measuring cups and spoons
Melon baller
Mixing bowls of various sizes
Muffin pan (12 cups)
Paper cups
Pastry bag with round tip
Pastry brush
Plastic wrap
Potato masher
Pot holders
Rolling pin
Rubber and metal spatulas
Saucepans with lids
Sieve
Sifter
Skewers*
Skillet
Star-shaped cookie cutters
Tall glasses
Tea kettle
Toaster oven*
Toothpicks
Vegetable peeler*
Water balloons
Wax paper
Whisk
Wooden spoons

*Use these items with extreme caution. Definitely get an adult to assist you anytime you need to use them.

Go forth, young Jedi! May your Ice Sabers and other frozen treats delight your appetite, and may the Force always be with you!

Ice Sabers

Sith Ice Saber

Light your way through the dark side with this fruity ice pop.

INGREDIENTS

1/3	cup red fruit juice (your choice)
1	teaspoon lemon juice
1/3	cup water
2	teaspoons sugar
	Red food coloring

1. Place the juices, water, and sugar into a small saucepan and stir. Bring the mixture to a boil over medium-high heat, then reduce the heat to low and simmer for 5 minutes, stirring constantly.

2. Pour the mixture into a glass measuring cup. Add a few drops of food coloring and stir until the color is uniform. Allow the mixture to cool to room temperature.

3. Fill up each ice saber mold, leaving ⅛ inch of space at the top (see illustration). Snap the hilt handles onto the top of the molds, and place the molds toward the back of your freezer.

4. Freeze until solid, at least 2 hours or overnight.

5. To remove the ice pops from the molds, run them under hot tap water for 5 seconds on each side. Gently remove the pops by the hilt handles.

Makes 4 ice pops.

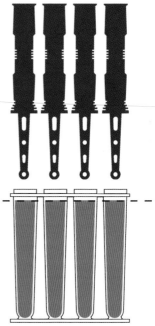

FILL MOLDS TO THE
DOTTED LINE INDICATED HERE

Obi-Wan's Ice Saber

The Jedi Master's signature blue lightsaber has never been so delicious.

INGREDIENTS

$1/3$	cup clear fruit juice, such as white grape or apple
$1/3$	cup water
2	teaspoons sugar
	Blue food coloring

1. Place the juice, water, and sugar into a small saucepan and stir. Bring the mixture to a boil over medium-high heat, then reduce the heat to low and simmer for 5 minutes, stirring constantly.

2. Pour the mixture into a glass measuring cup. Add a few drops of food coloring and stir until the color is uniform. Allow the mixture to cool to room temperature.

3. Fill up each ice saber mold, leaving ⅛ inch of space at the top (see illustration). Snap the hilt handles onto the top of the molds, and place the molds toward the back of your freezer.

4. Freeze until solid, at least 2 hours or overnight.

5. To remove the ice pops from the molds, run them under hot tap water for 5 seconds on each side. Gently remove the pops by the hilt handles.

Makes 4 ice pops.

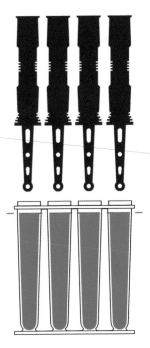

FILL MOLDS TO THE
DOTTED LINE INDICATED HERE
→

Luke's Ice Saber

This tart treat will please any Jedi.

INGREDIENTS

$1/3$	cup lime juice
$1/3$	cup water
4	teaspoons sugar
	Green food coloring

1. Place the juice, water, and sugar into a small saucepan and stir. Bring the mixture to a boil over medium-high heat, then reduce the heat to low and simmer for 5 minutes, stirring constantly.

2. Pour the mixture into a glass measuring cup. Add a few drops of food coloring and stir until the color is uniform. Allow the mixture to cool to room temperature.

3. Fill up each ice saber mold, leaving ⅛-inch of space at the top (see illustration). Snap the hilt handles onto the top of the molds, and place the molds toward the back of your freezer.

4. Freeze until solid, at least 2 hours or overnight.

5. To remove the ice pops from the molds, run them under hot tap water for 5 seconds on each side. Gently remove the pops by the hilt handles.

Makes 4 ice pops.

FILL MOLDS TO THE
DOTTED LINE INDICATED HERE

Handheld Treats

Han Solo's Blaster 'Bobs

A blast of cold air turns ordinary fruit into a yummy frozen treat.

INGREDIENTS

Bananas (one 3-inch piece for each blaster)

Assorted fruit, cut into $3/4$-inch pieces, as needed:

$1/4$ cup cherries

$1/4$ cup grapes

$1/4$ cup strawberries

$1/4$ cup blueberries

$1/4$ cup chopped pineapple

$1/4$ cup raspberries

1. Thread a 3-inch slice of banana crosswise onto a 10-inch wooden skewer about 1 inch from one end of the fruit. Slide it to about two thirds of the way down the skewer. Fill the rest of the skewer on either side with the remaining fruit pieces.

2. Break another skewer in half, and place it into the bottom of the banana to make the handle of the blaster. Fill the rest of the smaller skewer with fruit.

3. Repeat with the remaining fruit and place the filled skewers on a parchment- or wax paper–lined baking sheet. Freeze for at least 1 hour before serving, or cover with plastic wrap to freeze longer.

Makes 3 blasters.

Chewie Chocolate Cheesecake Pops

A fun way to eat a favorite treat!

CHOCOLATE CHEESECAKE

1	pound cream cheese, at room temperature
$^2/_3$	cup sugar
1	teaspoon vanilla extract
1	cup (6 ounces) chopped dark chocolate, melted and cooled
2	eggs

DIPPING CHOCOLATE

2	cups (12 ounces) chopped dark chocolate
$^1/_4$	cup vegetable shortening

1. Preheat the oven to 350°F.

2. To make the cheesecake: In a large bowl with an electric mixer, or in the bowl of a food processor, mix together the cream cheese, sugar, and vanilla on high until combined. Add the chocolate and combine until the mixture is well blended and uniform in color. Add the eggs one at a time, continuing to mix after each addition.

3. Scrape the mixture into an 8-inch square pan and bake for 35 to 45 minutes, until the filling is set. Set the pan on a cooling rack to cool completely, then transfer it to the freezer for 1 hour or overnight.

4. To make the dipping chocolate: Melt the 2 cups chocolate in the microwave or in the top of a double boiler. Add the shortening and stir until combined.

5. Cut the cheesecake into twenty-four rectangles: Cut twice across the pan to divide it into three even rows. Then, cut lengthwise once down the center to make two columns. Cut each column down its center again to make four columns. Cut each column down its center to make eight columns. Keep the pan in the refrigerator, removing three squares at a time to work with.

[continued]

6. Dip the top of a lollipop stick into the melted chocolate, and then insert it into the cheesecake square about halfway through. Then dip the cheesecake square into the chocolate, allowing the excess chocolate to drip off by tapping the stick on the side of the bowl. Set the stick in a block of Styrofoam, or lay it down on a sheet of wax paper. Repeat with the remaining cheesecake squares.

7. Place the dipped cheesecake squares in the freezer for at least 15 minutes before serving. Serve cold.

Makes 24 cheesecake pops.

Carbonite Delights

Freeze a mini Han Solo into a shell of chocolate.

BROWNIES

Two	1-ounce squares unsweetened chocolate
6	tablespoons butter
1	cup packed brown sugar
1	egg
1	teaspoon vanilla extract
1/2	cup all-purpose flour

2	pints vanilla ice cream
12	Tootsie Rolls

CHOCOLATE SHELL

3	cups (18 ounces) chopped semisweet chocolate
6	tablespoons vegetable shortening

1. Preheat the oven to 350°F.

2. To make the brownies: Line a 7-x-11-inch pan with aluminum foil, leaving a 1-inch overhang on the two long sides. Lightly grease the foil liner.

3. Melt the unsweetened chocolate and butter over medium heat in a medium saucepan, stirring until the mixture is well blended and smooth. Remove the saucepan from the heat. Add the sugar and mix to combine. Add the egg and vanilla and stir until incorporated. Add in the flour and stir until mixed in completely.

4. Spread the batter into the prepared pan. Bake for 15 to 20 minutes, or until the edges are firm and a cake tester inserted in the center comes out clean. Place the pan on a rack until cooled completely.

5. Move the ice cream to the refrigerator to soften while the brownies are cooling.

6. Spread the ice cream over the brownie crust, smoothing it evenly with a rubber spatula. Freeze it for at least 1 hour.

[continued]

7. While the brownie and ice cream combination is freezing, make each of the Tootsie Rolls into mini Han Solos: If the rolls are very stiff, soften them in the microwave for 5 to 10 seconds. Form the top into a round head, then flatten the rest of the Tootsie Roll, and use a knife to slice out legs and arms. Raise the arms and form hands at the ends.

8. To make the chocolate shell: Melt the semisweet chocolate in the microwave or in the top of a double boiler. Add the shortening and stir until melted and smooth.

9. Lift the ice cream and brownie from the pan by the edges of the foil and cut it into twelve pieces with a large, sharp knife. Press one of the Han Solos into each brownie piece, lay them on a baking sheet, and return them to the freezer. Working with one piece at a time, hold the square by the brownie portion and dip the entire piece into the melted chocolate, coating the ice cream entirely, until the coating comes up to the edge of the brownie. Tap the brownie on the side of the bowl to remove excess chocolate. Return the coated square to the freezer and repeat with the remaining squares. Freeze for at least 1 hour before serving.

Makes 12 ice cream treats.

Butterscotch Banana Battle Droids

These pops are prepared to do battle against snack-time hunger!

INGREDIENTS

4   small bananas, cut in half crosswise

One   11-ounce bag butterscotch chips

6   tablespoons vegetable shortening

Mini chocolate chips, mini colored chocolate candies, small round black sprinkles, or food coloring pen for decorating

1. Insert an ice-pop stick into each banana half, about one third of the way from the cut end. Place the bananas in the freezer for 2 hours or overnight.
2. Melt the butterscotch chips in the microwave or in the top of a double boiler. Add the shortening and stir until combined. Dip the frozen bananas in the butterscotch, covering the entire bananas and letting the excess butterscotch drip off by tapping the sticks on the side of the bowl. To make eyes, place two mini chocolate chips or candies on each banana while the coating is still wet. Set the sticks in a block of Styrofoam. (If using a food coloring pen, decorate the pops once the coating has set.)
3. Return the pops to the freezer for at least 1 hour before serving.
Makes 8 pops.

Lan-Dough Cookie Dough

These deep, dark chocolate cookies can be baked on the fly.

INGREDIENTS

2   cups all-purpose flour

$3/4$ cup unsweetened cocoa powder

$1/2$ teaspoon baking soda

$1/2$ teaspoon salt

$1/2$ cup (1 stick) butter, at room temperature

1   cup granulated sugar, plus additional for sprinkling

1   cup packed brown sugar

1   egg

1   teaspoon vanilla extract

1. In a large bowl, mix together the flour, cocoa powder, baking soda, and salt and set aside.

2. In a medium bowl, using an electric mixer on medium speed, cream together the butter and sugars until fluffy. Beat in the egg and vanilla. Gradually add the dry ingredients until a stiff dough forms.

3. Separate the dough into two 12-inch logs. Sprinkle a sheet of wax paper with additional sugar and roll each of the logs to coat. Wrap each log well in plastic wrap and freeze at least 4 hours or overnight.

4. Preheat the oven to 350°F.

5. Cut each log into 48 slices. Place the slices at least 1 inch apart on lightly greased baking sheets. Bake for 10 to 12 minutes, or until the tops look dry (the middles will still be soft). Remove the cookies to a wire rack to cool.

Makes 8 dozen cookies.

Qui-Gon Gingerbread Sandwiches

Sweet and spicy sammies for the Jedi on the go!

INGREDIENTS

4	cups all-purpose flour
3	teaspoons pumpkin pie spice
1	teaspoon baking soda
1/2	teaspoon salt
1/2	cup (1 stick) butter, at room temperature
1/2	cup packed brown sugar
1/2	cup dark molasses
1	pint dulce de leche or caramel swirl ice cream

1. Preheat the oven to 350°F.
2. In a large bowl, whisk together the flour, pie spice, baking soda, and salt. Set aside.
3. In a medium bowl, with an electric mixer on medium speed, cream together the butter and sugar until fluffy. Add the molasses and beat until well combined. Add one third of the flour mixture and 1 tablespoon water alternately (4 tablespoons water total), mixing well after each addition. If the dough is dry or doesn't hold together well, add an additional tablespoon of water to the mixture.
4. Gather the dough and roll it out to fit onto an 11-x-15-inch jelly-roll pan. Bake it for 8 to 10 minutes, until the dough springs back when pressed lightly with the back of a spoon. Cool it completely on a cooling rack.
5. Move the ice cream to the refrigerator to soften while the dough is cooling.
6. Cut out 16 cookies with a 2-inch cookie cutter. Lay the cookie cutter on a flat surface and press in one of the cookies to the bottom. Fill the cookie cutter with ice cream, then top it with another cookie. Press the top down to gently remove the sandwich from the cookie cutter. Repeat with the remaining cookies and ice cream. Wrap each sandwich in plastic wrap and freeze them for at least 1 hour before serving.

Makes 8 ice cream sandwiches.

Tauntaun Bon Bons

Even Tauntauns deserve a treat! These frozen balls of ice creamy delectability are easy to make, and keep well for last-minute guests.

INGREDIENTS

1	pint vanilla ice cream
1	cup crushed peppermint candies (about 30 candies)
1	cup crushed vanilla sandwich cookies (about 25 cookies)

1. Using a melon baller or small ice-cream scoop, scoop out 16 small, round balls of ice cream. Place the scoops onto a parchment-lined baking sheet in the freezer as you work. Freeze the scoops for 3 hours.
2. Mix together the cookie crumbs and candy in a shallow dish. Remove two or three scoops of ice cream from the freezer at a time and roll them in the candy and cookie mixture to make the bon bons. Return the covered bon bons to the tray in the freezer, and repeat with the remaining scoops.
3. When all of the ice cream has been covered with the cookie and candy mixture, freeze it for another hour and then serve, or transfer the bon bons to an airtight container and freeze for up to 1 month.
Makes approximately 16 bon bons.

Cakes and Pies

Millennium Fal-Cone Pie

Blast off for deliciousness with this crunchy, creamy pie. Shape a disposable pie pan like Han Solo's ship by slightly bending the sides and squaring off the front.

CRUST

9	sugar ice cream cones
1/4	cup (1/2 stick) butter, melted
1	tablespoon sugar
1	quart ice cream (flavor of your choice), softened for 15 to 20 minutes on the counter

SUGAR CONE CRUNCH

3	sugar ice cream cones
2	tablespoons sugar
1	tablespoon butter

1. Preheat the oven to 350°F.
2. To make the crust: In the bowl of a food processor, add the 9 sugar cones and pulse until they become crumbs. Add the butter and sugar and pulse 3 to 4 times, until the cones are completely coated.
3. Pour the crumb mixture into a 9-inch pie pan and press it against the bottom and up the sides, pressing well to make a firm, compact crust.
4. Bake for 5 minutes to set the crust. Remove from the oven and cool completely.
5. Fill the crust with the ice cream, smoothing the top. Put it in the freezer.
6. To make the sugar cone crunch: In a plastic zipper bag, crush the sugar cones into 1/2-inch pieces and set aside. In a small saucepan, combine the sugar with 2 tablespoons water and stir gently until the sugar is dissolved. Bring the mixture to a boil over medium-high heat. Continue to boil, without stirring, until the syrup is golden and a candy thermometer reads 250°F, about 6 to 8 minutes. Remove the syrup from the heat, add the butter, and stir to combine. Immediately add the crushed sugar cones and stir to coat completely.
7. Transfer the coated sugar cones to a sheet of wax paper or a nonstick pan liner. Spread the mixture into an even layer and allow it to cool completely.
8. When the sugar cone crunch is cool, place it in the zipper bag and use a rolling pin to roll over it, crushing it into small, equal-size pieces.
9. Sprinkle the sugar cone crunch evenly over the top of the pie, pressing in lightly. Freeze for 1 hour or overnight.
10. To serve, allow the pie to thaw for 10 to 15 minutes in the refrigerator, then slice it with a knife that has been dipped in hot water and wiped off with a dish towel. Wrap leftovers with plastic and refreeze.
Makes 8 to 10 servings.

Darth Chocolate Mud Pie

This rich chocolaty pie might just lure you over to the dark side.

CRUST

20	chocolate sandwich cookies
2	tablespoons butter, melted
1	quart chocolate ice cream, softened for 15 to 20 minutes on the counter

One 4-ounce block dark chocolate, at room temperature

CHOCOLATE SAUCE

1	cup (6 ounces) chopped semisweet chocolate
3/4	cup heavy whipping cream

1. Preheat the oven to 350°F.

2. To make the crust: In the bowl of a food processor, pulse the cookies until they become fine crumbs. Add the butter and pulse 3 to 4 times, until the cookies are completely coated.

3. Pour the crumb mixture into a 9-inch pie pan and press it against the bottom and up the sides, pressing well to make a firm, compact crust.

4. Bake for 10 minutes to set the crust. Remove it from the oven and cool completely.

5. Fill the crust with the ice cream, smoothing the top. Put it in the freezer.

6. Hold the block of chocolate with a paper towel to prevent the heat of your hand from melting the chocolate. Firmly draw a vegetable peeler across the chocolate and let the curls drop onto a sheet of wax paper. Continue until you have enough curls to cover the surface of the pie, about ¾ cup. Chill the curls in the refrigerator for 15 to 20 minutes to firm, then place them evenly over the surface of the pie. Return the pie to the freezer for at least 1 hour or overnight.

7. To make the sauce: Combine the chocolate and cream in a medium glass or ceramic bowl. Microwave for 2 minutes, until the chocolate is soft and the cream is warm, then whisk to combine completely. Allow the sauce to cool and thicken for 10 to 15 minutes and then serve it immediately, or make it ahead and chill and reheat to serve.

8. To serve, allow the pie to thaw for 10 to 15 minutes in the refrigerator, then slice it with a knife that has been dipped in hot water and wiped off with a dish towel, and top with the sauce. Wrap leftovers with plastic and refreeze.

Makes 8 to 10 servings.

Rollies

"Rollies" is slang for the fast—very fast—droidekas, or destroyer droids. This yummy cake will disappear fast—very fast—from the plates of anyone you serve it to.

INGREDIENTS

Vegetable-oil cooking spray

1 cup all-purpose flour

1/3 cup plus 1 tablespoon unsweetened cocoa powder

1 teaspoon baking powder

1/2 teaspoon salt

4 eggs

3/4 cup granulated sugar

1 teaspoon vanilla extract

2 tablespoons confectioners' sugar

1 quart coffee ice cream, softened for 15 to 20 minutes on the counter

1. Preheat the oven to 350°F degrees.
2. Line an 11-x-15-inch jelly-roll pan with parchment or wax paper. Spray the paper and sides of the pan with the oil spray.
3. In a medium bowl, mix together the flour, 1/3 cup of the cocoa powder, the baking powder, and salt in a medium bowl, and set aside.
4. In a large bowl, using an electric mixer on high, beat the eggs until they are very light, about 5 minutes. Gradually add the granulated sugar, beating until smooth. Mix in the vanilla and stir until combined.
5. Fold the dry ingredients into the egg mixture until fully incorporated and free of lumps. Spread the batter evenly into the prepared pan. Bake for 12 to 15 minutes, or until the cake springs back when touched.
6. While the cake is baking, mix the confectioners' sugar with the remaining 1 tablespoon cocoa powder in a small bowl. Spread a clean dish towel on a flat counter or table and sprinkle it liberally with the sugar-cocoa mixture. When the cake is done, turn it out immediately onto the prepared towel. Roll up the towel and cake loosely from a short end. Place it seam-side down on a wire rack and cool completely.
7. When the cake is cool, unroll it and spread it with the ice cream to 1 inch from the edges. Reroll the cake and wrap it tightly with plastic wrap. Freeze it at least 4 hours or overnight. To serve, let the cake thaw on the counter for 10 to 15 minutes and slice it with a serrated knife. Rewrap and freeze any leftovers.
Makes 10 servings.

Frozen Yodagurt Cake

Delicious, this is. Tint a homemade angel food cake green to give it a Yoda-like hue, or use a store-bought angel food cake and tint the softened frozen yogurt!

CAKE

1 cup cake flour

$^1/_4$ teaspoon salt

12 large egg whites, at room temperature

1 teaspoon cream of tartar

1$^1/_4$ cups sugar

2 teaspoons vanilla extract

1 teaspoon green food coloring

FILLING

1 quart frozen yogurt (any flavor), softened for 15 to 20 minutes on the counter

1 cup sliced fresh strawberries

1. Preheat the oven to 350°F.

2. To make the cake: Sift the flour and salt into a medium bowl and set aside.

3. In a medium bowl, with an electric mixer on medium speed, beat the egg whites until foamy. Add the cream of tartar and increase the speed to high, continuing to beat until soft peaks form. Gradually add the sugar while beating, until the peaks become stiff. Beat in the vanilla and food coloring.

4. Sift one quarter of the flour mixture over the egg whites and gently fold the mixture in until completely combined. Repeat three more times with the remaining flour mixture.

5. Transfer the batter to an ungreased 10-inch tube pan and smooth the top with a spatula. Bake for 30 to 40 minutes, until the top is golden and springs back when touched. Invert the pan on a cooling rack and let cool at room temperature for at least 1 hour. Run a knife around the sides of the cake to release it from the pan.

6. To assemble the cake: With a serrated bread knife, cut the cake in half crosswise. Slice each half in half again to make four layers in all. Place the bottom later on a flat serving plate. Spread the layer with 1 cup of the yogurt and then one quarter of the sliced strawberries. Repeat with the remaining cake layers, yogurt, and berries.

7. Serve immediately, or wrap the cake in plastic wrap and freeze. To serve it from frozen, allow the cake to thaw on the counter for 10 to 15 minutes and slice it with a serrated knife. Wrap leftovers with plastic and refreeze.

Makes 8 to 10 servings.

Princess Leia's Lemon Soufflé

Like Leia, this treat is cool and tart but also sweet.

INGREDIENTS

6	eggs, separated
1	cup sugar
3	large lemons, zested and juiced
1/4	teaspoon cream of tartar
1 1/2	cups heavy whipping cream

1. Place the egg yolks, sugar, lemon juice, and zest in a medium saucepan and cook over medium-high heat, stirring constantly, until the mixture has thickened and there are small bubbles just around the edges, about 5 to 7 minutes.

2. Strain the mixture into a large glass bowl. Place plastic wrap directly on the surface of the mixture and refrigerate until cold, at least 30 minutes or overnight.

3. In a medium bowl, with an electric mixer, beat the egg whites with the cream of tartar until stiff peaks form. Mix a dollop of egg white into the lemon mixture to lighten it, then fold in the rest of the egg whites.

4. In the same bowl, beat the cream until stiff peaks form, then fold it into the lemon mixture.

5. Transfer the soufflé mixture to a 9- or 10-inch springform pan, and smooth the top with a spatula. Freeze it until firm, 6 hours or overnight.

6. To serve, remove the sides of the springform pan and slice the soufflé with a knife that has been dipped in hot water and wiped clean. Wrap leftovers with plastic and refreeze.

Makes 8 to 10 servings.

Ice Cream, Sherbet, and Sundaes

Bananakin Splits

STRAWBERRY SAUCE

One 12-ounce bag frozen
strawberries

$1/4$ cup granulated sugar

1 teaspoon fresh lemon
juice

ROASTED BANANAS

4 ripe bananas, peeled and
halved lengthwise

2 tablespoons brown sugar

CHOCOLATE SAUCE

$1/2$ cup heavy whipping cream

$3/4$ cup ($4^1/2$ ounces) chopped
semisweet chocolate

SPLITS

1 pint each of chocolate,
vanilla, and strawberry
ice cream

$1/2$ cup crushed pineapple

Whipped cream

12 maraschino cherries

1. To make the strawberry sauce: Set the strawberries in a fine strainer over a bowl and thaw for several hours or in the refrigerator overnight. Reserve the juice in a small bowl and set aside. Force the berries through the strainer with a wooden spoon, mashing and stirring until as much of the berry puree as possible is passed through the strainer. Discard the seeds. Add the reserved juice, granulated sugar, and lemon juice and stir to combine.

2. Preheat the oven to 400°F.

3. To make the roasted bananas: Line a baking sheet with parchment paper or a nonstick liner. Place the bananas on the prepared sheet, cut-side up. Sprinkle the tops with the brown sugar. Roast for 30 minutes, or until the bananas are soft when tested with a fork and the topping is golden and bubbly. Cool for 15 minutes.

4. To make the chocolate sauce: Melt the cream and chocolate together in a microwave or in the top of a double boiler. Stir until smooth. Set aside. It will thicken as it cools.

5. To make the splits: Put one scoop each of the chocolate, vanilla, and strawberry ice cream into four long ice cream split bowls.

6. Top the vanilla ice cream with the chocolate sauce, the strawberry ice cream with the crushed pineapple, and the chocolate ice cream with the strawberry sauce. Add two banana slices to each split and top with the whipped cream and cherries.

Makes 4 splits.

Ewoki Road Sundaes

TOFFEE GRAHAM CRACKERS

4 graham crackers, full sheets

$1^1/_2$ tablespoons brown sugar

$1^1/_2$ tablespoons butter

1 pint chocolate ice cream

MARSHMALLOW SAUCE

$^1/_3$ cup granulated sugar

2 tablespoons corn syrup

1 cup miniature marshmallows

1 teaspoon vanilla extract

1. Preheat the oven to 350°F.

2. To make the toffee graham crackers: Lay the crackers on a baking sheet touching edge to edge.

3. In a small saucepan over medium heat, stir together the brown sugar and butter and bring them to a boil. Stir constantly while boiling for 2 minutes. Turn off the heat and immediately pour the syrup over the graham crackers, spreading it evenly with a knife or spatula.

4. Bake the crackers for 5 minutes, until the topping is bubbly. Remove the pan from the oven and cool completely in the pan on a rack.

5. Scoop the ice cream into four bowls and place them in the freezer while you prepare the marshmallow sauce.

6. To make the marshmallow sauce: Bring the granulated sugar, 2 table-spoons water, and the corn syrup to a boil in a small saucepan over medium-high heat, stirring constantly. Reduce the heat and simmer for 4 minutes, stirring occasionally.

7. Remove the syrup from the heat and add the marshmallows and vanilla. Stir until smooth. Let cool. (This marshmallow sauce is best if used right away.)

8. To serve, top the ice cream with the sauce and crumble a toffee graham cracker over each sundae.

Makes 4 sundaes.

R2-D2ti Fruity Sundaes

RASPBERRY SAUCE

One 12-ounce bag frozen raspberries

1/4 cup sugar

1 teaspoon fresh lemon juice

1 pint strawberry ice cream

1/2 cup blueberries, fresh or frozen

Whipped cream

1. To make the raspberry sauce: Set the raspberries in a fine strainer over a bowl and thaw for several hours or in the refrigerator overnight. Reserve the juice in a small bowl and set aside. Force the berries through the strainer with a wooden spoon, mashing and stirring until as much of the berry puree as possible is passed through the strainer. Discard the seeds. Add the reserved juice, sugar, and lemon juice and stir to combine.
2. To make the sundaes: Scoop the ice cream into four bowls. Top with the raspberry sauce, blueberries, and whipped cream.
Makes 4 sundaes.

Wookiee Cookie Bowls

These sweet, edible bowls are perfect for holding your favorite ice cream, mousse, or pudding.

INGREDIENTS

$^1/_2$ cup (1 stick) butter, at room temperature

$^1/_2$ cup sugar

1   egg

1   teaspoon vanilla extract

$1^1/_3$ cups all-purpose flour

1   teaspoon baking powder

$^1/_4$ teaspoon salt

1. Preheat the oven to 350°F.

2. In a medium bowl, with an electric mixer on high, cream together the butter and sugar until fluffy. Add the egg and vanilla and mix to combine.

3. In a medium bowl, whisk together the flour, baking powder, and salt. Add the dry ingredients to the butter mixture ½ cup at a time, mixing completely after each addition.

4. Turn the dough onto a floured surface and knead it a few times until smooth. Roll out the dough to ⅛ inch thick, sprinkling it with flour as needed. Cut it into 4-inch rounds, using a large clean, empty can or cut a template from paper and trace around it with a small, sharp knife.

5. Turn a 12-cup muffin pan upside-down and drape each of the rounds over the cups, pressing gently. Bake for 12 to 15 minutes, or until golden.

6. Cool the cups on the muffin pan for 10 minutes, then gently remove each one to a rack to cool completely. Store in an airtight container for up to a week.

Makes 12 cookie bowls.

Ice Cream Clones

Inspired by the Clone Troopers created to serve the Grand Army of the Republic, these frozen treats will march forth from your freezer to attack your mouth with deliciousness. Follow the example in the photo to replicate the Clone Trooper's helmet.

INGREDIENTS

4   flat-bottomed, plain cake ice cream cones

1   pint vanilla ice cream, softened for 15 to 20 minutes on the counter

COATING

1   cup (6 ounces) chopped white chocolate

$1/4$ cup coconut oil

$1/4$ cup dark chocolate or food coloring pen for decorating

1. Fill the ice cream cones with ½-cup scoops of ice cream. Freeze them for 1 hour.

2. To make the coating: Melt the white chocolate with the coconut oil in a microwave or the top of a double boiler and stir until completely combined.

3. Remove one filled ice cream cone from the freezer. Smooth the ice cream with the palm of your hand. Dip the cone into the coating to the edge of the cone. Return the dipped cone to the freezer and dip the rest of the cones.

4. To melt the chocolate for piping: Place the chocolate in a heavy glass or ceramic measuring cup and microwave for 1 minute on 50% power. Stir, and heat again at 30-second intervals until the chocolate is smooth and melted.

5. Decorate the cones with the melted dark chocolate, piped with a pastry bag, following the pattern on the clone helmets. Alternatively, you may decorate with a food coloring pen.

Makes 4 cones.

AT-AT Tracks

Moose Tracks is a popular ice cream flavor, but there are no moose in galaxies far, far away. An AT-AT (All-Terrain Armored Transport) makes impressive tracks, and these sundaes have chocolate and peanut butter flavors that capture the terrestrial inspiration.

CHOCOLATE-PEANUT BUTTER SAUCE

$^1/_2$	cup heavy whipping cream
$^1/_2$	cup (3 ounces) chopped semisweet chocolate
2	tablespoons smooth peanut butter

1	pint vanilla ice cream
4	large peanut butter cups, chopped
	Whipped cream and chopped peanuts (optional)

1. To make the sauce: Melt the chocolate and cream together in the microwave or in the top of a double boiler. Stir until smooth. Add the peanut butter and stir until smooth.

2. Scoop the ice cream into four bowls. Top with the sauce and chopped peanut butter cups. Add a dollop of whipped cream and sprinkle on the chopped peanuts, if desired.

Makes 4 sundaes.

Bantha Bowls

INGREDIENTS

2   cups (12 ounces) chopped semisweet chocolate

1   tablespoon shortening or coconut oil (optional)

    Vegetable-oil cooking spray

1. Melt the chocolate in the microwave for 1 minute, stir, then microwave and stir at 30-second intervals until it is melted and smooth. If you're using chocolate chips or the chocolate is very thick, add the shortening or coconut oil and stir until smooth.

2. Blow up 8 small, brightly colored water balloon–sized balloons about three quarters full and tie them closed. Spray your hands with a little oil and rub the bottoms and halfway up the balloons with oil. Line a baking sheet with parchment or wax paper.

3. Dip the bottom of each balloon in the melted chocolate about 2 inches up the sides. Remove it from the chocolate and place it on the baking sheet. Let the balloons sit until the chocolate has hardened, about 45 minutes.

4. Once the chocolate is dry and hard, prick the top of each balloon right near the knot with a needle or pin. Let the balloons slowly deflate. Remove the balloons and fill the chocolate cups with your favorite ice cream. Make sure to check again when you fill the bowls that there are no traces of balloons left in the bowl. You may store the bowls, covered, in the refrigerator for up to a week.

Makes 8 bowls.

Mos Icely

The rounded tops of these refreshing citrus cups look like the rounded buildings of the Mos Eisley spaceport where Luke, Obi-Wan, and the droids stopped in at the cantina for a little drink—and a lot of trouble.

INGREDIENTS

6   large oranges

$1/2$ cup sugar

$1/4$ cup fresh lemon juice

1. Slice the tops of the oranges about one third of the way from the top and scoop out all of the flesh into a fine sieve set over a large bowl. Put the empty orange peel "cups" on a baking sheet in the freezer.
2. Mash the orange pulp with the back of a wooden spoon to extract as much juice as possible, about 1½ cups.
3. Combine the sugar and 1 cup water in a medium saucepan over medium heat and simmer until the sugar is dissolved. Raise the heat to medium-high and boil for 5 minutes. Add the juices, stir, and cool.
4. When the juice mixture is cool, pour it into a shallow baking pan, cover with plastic wrap, and freeze for 1 to 2 hours, until the mixture is frozen hard at the edges. Scrape it with a fork from the edges to the center. Return to the freezer and repeat two or three more times at 20-minutes intervals, until the granita is uniformly icy.
5. To serve, scoop the granita into the frozen orange cups.
Makes 6 servings.

Asteroid Attack

When these asteroids come hurling toward you, open up and let the crisp warm crust and cool creamy ice cream blast your mouth with yumminess.

INGREDIENTS

1   quart vanilla ice cream, softened for 15 to 20 minutes on the counter

CRUST

1   cup crushed corn flake cereal

$1/2$ cup sweetened shredded coconut

$1/2$ cup graham cracker crumbs (about 7 crackers)

3   large egg whites

    Vegetable oil for frying

    Whipped cream and chocolate sauce for serving (optional)

1. Scoop the ice cream into eight ½-cup balls. Place them on a baking sheet and freeze for at least 1 hour.

2. To make the crust: Combine the cereal, coconut, and cracker crumbs in a shallow bowl. In another shallow bowl, beat the egg whites with a fork until combined.

3. One by one, remove the ice cream scoops from the freezer and roll them in the egg whites and then in the cereal mixture. Repeat until all of the ice cream scoops are covered. Return the coated scoops to the freezer. Freeze for 1 hour or cover with plastic wrap to freeze longer.

4. When ready to serve, heat enough oil to cover the balls in a large, heavy pot or deep fryer to 400°F. Working with two scoops at a time, place them on a slotted spoon and carefully lower them into the oil. Fry until golden, about 30 to 60 seconds. Remove with a slotted spoon and place them in dessert cups. Top with whipped cream and chocolate sauce, if desired. Repeat with the remaining scoops.

Makes 8 servings.

Twin Suns Sherbet Bombe

This fruity treat mirrors the twin suns as they rise over the Tatooine horizon.

INGREDIENTS

1	pint orange sherbet
2	pints vanilla ice cream, softened for 15 to 20 minutes on the counter
1	cup crushed amaretti cookies (about 20 small cookies)

1. Freeze a 9-x-5-inch metal loaf pan for 30 minutes.

2. While the pan is freezing, use a melon baller to make 14 small scoops of orange sherbet. Freeze the scoops on a baking sheet for 15 minutes.

3. Remove the chilled pan from the freezer and fill it with the remaining sherbet. Freeze it for 15 minutes. Remove the pan from the freezer, and layer it with half of the vanilla ice cream. Place the sherbet balls in two rows down the length of the pan. Return the pan to the freezer for 15 minutes. Remove it and add the rest of the vanilla ice cream, smoothing the top with a rubber spatula. Scatter the crushed cookies over the top and press them in lightly. Freeze for 2 hours or overnight.

4. To serve, invert the pan onto a chilled plate. Soak a dish towel in hot water, wring it dry, and cover the outside of the pan for 1 to 2 minutes. Gently lift the pan from the ice cream.

5. Slice the bombe every ¾ to 1 inch with a knife that has been dipped in hot water. Wipe the knife with a dish towel between each slice.

Makes 10 to 12 servings.

Tatooine Terrine

The nutty top of this delicious dessert resembles the sandy landscape of Luke Skywalker's home planet.

INGREDIENTS

2	cups (12 ounces) chopped milk or dark chocolate
1	cup smooth peanut butter
1	teaspoon vanilla extract
1	cup heavy whipping cream
$^1/_4$	cup sugar
1	cup chopped roasted peanuts

1. Line the inside of a 9-x-5-inch loaf pan with plastic wrap, leaving enough overhang to wrap the finished terrine.

2. Melt the chocolate in a medium metal bowl over a double boiler. Add the peanut butter and vanilla and whisk to blend. Remove the bowl from the heat and set it aside to cool to room temperature.

3. In a medium bowl, with an electric mixer on high, whip the cream until foamy. Gradually add the sugar while continuing to whip, until stiff peaks form. Fold in the cooled chocolate mixture.

4. Sprinkle ½ cup of the peanuts on the bottom of the prepared loaf pan. Pour the chocolate mixture into the pan and smooth it with a rubber spatula. Sprinkle the top evenly with the remaining peanuts. Wrap the ends of the plastic wrap firmly over the filled pan and press lightly.

5. Freeze for at least 3 hours or overnight.

6. To remove the terrine from the pan, unwrap the plastic wrap to expose the top layer and invert the pan onto a serving platter. Remove the pan and the plastic wrap. To serve, slice the terrine with a serrated knife that has been dipped in hot water. Wipe the knife with a dish towel between each slice.

Makes 10 to 12 servings.

Beverages

Echo Base Frozen Lemonade

Echo Base is a Rebel military outpost on the icy planet Hoth. When soldiers return from patrol, they can relax with this refreshing drink.

INGREDIENTS

1	cup sugar
	Rinds of 5 lemons (yellow skin only, no white pith)
1	cup fresh lemon juice (from the lemons)

1. Combine 2 cups water, the sugar, and lemon rind in a saucepan and simmer for 10 to 15 minutes, stirring occasionally. Strain out the rind and add the lemon juice to the syrup. Cool to room temperature, then transfer the mixture to a glass baking dish. Cover and freeze for at least 4 hours or overnight.

2. To serve, break up the frozen lemonade with a fork and transfer the chunks to a food processor or blender. Pulse a few times until the mixture is slushy, then transfer to chilled glasses.

Makes 3 to 4 servings.

Ice Cream Yoda

Green mint ice cream and frothy brown chocolate soda are swirled together to recreate the mossy, swampy landscape of Yoda's home of Dagobah. If you're feeling generous, plunk in two straws and share with a friend.

INGREDIENTS

3	tablespoons chocolate syrup
1	tablespoon milk or cream
1	cup seltzer water or club soda
2	generous scoops mint chip ice cream
	Whipped cream for serving (optional)

Measure the chocolate syrup and milk into the bottom of a tall glass. While stirring with a fork, slowly add ¾ cup of the seltzer and mix until combined. Add the ice cream and top with the rest of the seltzer and the whipped cream, if desired.
Makes 1 to 2 servings.

Frozen Hoth Chocolate

Everything on the ice planet Hoth is cold and icy—
even the hot chocolate. This treat is perfect for relax-
ing after a long day of tramping through the snow on
a tauntaun.

INGREDIENTS

2^1/$_2$ cups plus 2 tablespoons milk

^{3}/4 cup sugar

^{1}/$_2$ cup unsweetened cocoa powder

 Whipped cream and chocolate shavings for garnish (optional)

1. In a medium saucepan, whisk together 2½ cups of the milk, the
sugar, and cocoa powder, then simmer until the sugar is dissolved, about
10 minutes. Remove from the heat and allow the mixture to cool, then
pour it into an 8-inch square baking pan. Freeze for about 2 hours, stir
with a fork, then return it to the freezer for 4 more hours or overnight.
2. When ready to serve, transfer the frozen mixture to a food processor
with the remaining 2 tablespoons milk and pulse several times until
smooth and slushy. Serve in chilled glasses with whipped cream and
chocolate shavings, if desired.
Makes 3 to 4 servings.

Cloud City Ice Cream Floats

Lando Calrissian invited Han, Luke, and Leia to dine at his home on Cloud City. Unfortunately, Darth Vader was also a guest and the crew never had a chance to eat. These delicious floats that look like fluffy clouds in a night sky would've been a perfect way to end the meal that never was . . . .

BLUEBERRY SYRUP

2	cups fresh or frozen blueberries, thawed
1/2	cup sugar
1	tablespoon fresh lemon juice

ICE CREAM FLOATS

1/2	cup blueberry syrup (or use store-bought syrup)
2	cups seltzer water or club soda
4	scoops vanilla ice cream

1. To make the syrup: In a small saucepan, simmer the blueberries and 1 cup water for 15 minutes, stirring frequently. Strain through a fine-mesh sieve, pressing out as much of the juice as possible with the back of a wooden spoon. Return the juice to the saucepan and add the sugar and lemon juice. Bring to a boil over medium-high heat and stir until the sugar is dissolved, about 2 to 3 minutes. Transfer the syrup to a glass measuring cup and cool to room temperature. Store covered in the refrigerator for up to 2 weeks.

2. To make the floats: Fill the bottoms of two tall, chilled glasses with ¼ cup blueberry syrup each. Add ¾ cup seltzer to each glass and stir until combined. Add 2 scoops vanilla ice cream to each glass, and top with the remaining seltzer.

Makes 2 servings.

Index